THE PERFECT
ENGLISH COUNTRY COTTAGE

THE PERFECT
ENGLISH COUNTRY COTTAGE

Lydia Greeves

PHOTOGRAPHS BY JOHN MILLER

Thames and Hudson

ACKNOWLEDGMENTS

Lydia Greeves is very grateful to all those in the National Trust who provided information for this book, and to Sheila Mortimer for her unfailing support.

All the cottages featured in this book are now in the care of the National Trust, and some (those featuring the National Trust's oak-leaf symbol below the text) are available for rent. A brochure on the Trust's holiday cottages and further information can be obtained from National Trust Holiday Booking Office, PO Box 536, Melksham, Wiltshire, SN12 8SX, England (tel. 01225 791133).

Library of Congress Catalog Card Number: 94-60227
ISBN 0-500-01626-7

Typeset in Horley Old Style 11/14½pt
Printed and bound in Spain by Cayfosa

Frontispiece: Bird How, Eskdale
Opposite: Saxon Cottage, Steyning

——CONTENTS——

INTRODUCTION

T HE MORE urban and machine-bound our lives become, the more we seem to hanker after an idealized countryside, in which thatched cottages, hung with roses and honeysuckle, cluster round an ancient church in a landscape of winding lanes, hedged fields and gently swelling hills. Increasingly, as most of us lose touch with our rural origins, the country cottage has come to represent a safe, unchanging, untroubled way of life: a time when summers were always long, the grass was always green, and every afternoon could be lazed away in the sun.

Cottages appeal because of their scale – approachable, human-sized, unthreatening – because they are at one with their surroundings, and because they have often been built by eye, without the sharp outlines and pretensions of grand architecture, and have warped and bulged into an unbuttoned maturity. Romance and nostalgia need a patina of age and decay, which is why spruce renovation destroys a cottage's appeal.

Before the railway and canal age, when heavy materials could, for the first time, be moved easily round the country, the cottage was an unselfconscious response to place, built of local materials and reflecting regional traditions. Few cottages, though, are very old, or not as old as their owners often like to think. For centuries, all but the great lived in what today would be classed as huts or hovels, flimsy, single-storey, windowless constructions of wood and thatch, mud and turf, verminous and easily destroyed.

These insubstantial, chimneyless structures began to disappear in Tudor and Stuart times, when increasing prosperity and a breakdown in old manorial ties encouraged a wave of new building. Permanent houses constructed by craftsmen began to go up all over the country, and it is these buildings which have largely survived. Put up by the upwardly mobile, they were a mark of worldly success, but over the centuries, in line with rising expectations and living standards, their status declined. Some were demoted from house to cottage, or, like the decayed Cotswold manor lived in by the young Laurie Lee, their original grandeur subdivided. At the same time, and well into the nineteenth century, the poor continued to live in squalor. As with so much else, a cottage, and its associations, are in the eye of the beholder.

Like the landscapes into which they fit so well, cottage styles and materials are strongly regional, varying markedly over relatively short distances. Much of this variety has to do with Britain's complex geology, with whether a builder faced hard tough granite, crumbly soft sandstone or malleable clay, and with whether the land supported stands of building timber or thin acid moorland. But building designs were also affected by relative wealth and the hardening and endurance of local idiosyncracies. Those parts of the country that were most remote and least prosperous, such as deepest Wales and the Northumbrian hills, lagged a century or so behind in adopting innovations and improvements. Similarly, when vernacular traditions demanded a high degree of skill, as in the stone villages of the Cotswolds, and a craft was passed on from master to apprentice for generations, engrained techniques, such as the use of carved-stone drip-moulds over doors and windows, persisted for centuries.

The basic materials of cottage construction were mud, timber, stone and thatch. Mud, variously mixed with chopped straw, sand or gravel, and moulded into bricks or roughly laid, layer on layer, was within reach of even the poorest. More than any other material, though, it is intensely vulnerable. If cared for and kept dry it can last, but if neglected it decays rapidly; and it is structurally weak. Today, mud cottages survive only in those areas where, until comparatively recent times, there were no alternative building materials, notably in the enchanting cob villages of the West Country, and in the clay-lump buildings of East Anglia.

Until four hundred years ago, when the great forests which once carpeted much of the country began to be depleted, wood was the most popular and widely used material, with an important city such as London still being largely timber-built at the time of the Great Fire in 1666. Oak, strong, durable and hardening with time, was the preferred timber, and it was used green. It was the twisting and warping of the beams as they dried which has given so many cottages and houses an impression of great age.

In direct contrast to buildings of stone, brick or mud, all timber-framed houses are based on a structural skeleton, usually prepared beforehand in a workshop and then speedily erected on site. First, and simplest, is what is known as a cruck frame, in which the roof is carried on pairs of huge bent timbers which rest on the ground – or, more usually, on a damp-course of stone or brick – and come together at the apex of the building. Cottages constructed in this way are limited by the span and height of the crucks, which tend to enforce low-ceilinged, cramped upper floors, but this system of building, like modern steel-framing, gives a structure which is completely independent of the walls, and these can be renewed, moved or replaced without disturbing the roof.

More common is the type of structure in which the roof rests on the walls. Some cottages are built like timber boxes, fitted together piece by piece, with the weight of the roof taken on all the uprights; others are of post and truss construction, with some key uprights supporting the roof. Both systems are more flexible than the simple cruck, giving scope for buildings of some size and for the projecting upper floors which are such an attractive feature of many old houses. Timber-framed cottages of all varieties survive over large areas of England, but particularly in the once heavily wooded valleys of the Kent and Sussex Weald, in the clay lands of Suffolk and

Essex, and in the formerly timber-rich Welsh Borders and Midlands. Timber skeletons were originally infilled with wattle and daub, made by plastering hurdle-like panels of pliable twigs with a coating of mud mixed with straw and hair, but this infill has often been replaced by brick, known as brick-nogging.

Wood, like mud, is vulnerable to decay, and much of the regional variation in the appearance of timber-framed buildings stems from the way they are protected against the weather. Plastered, colour-washed cottages, some showing the stencil-like decoration known as pargetting, compose a series of delectable Suffolk villages; in Kent and Sussex you will see façades hung with warm red tiles, or with crisply white or tarred weather-boarding; while in the Welsh Borders the frame is not only left exposed, but is accentuated, standing out black against white in the magpie treatment characteristic of the region.

Stone buildings are more strongly regional, and take on the characteristics of the underlying rock in a way that means house and landscape are uniquely matched. Most desirable are the buildings of the limestone belt, which sweeps across England from Dorset to Yorkshire. Easily worked with hand tools, limestone lends itself to fine detail and smooth finishes, but it looks just as good in a licheny wall of roughly coursed rubble, or in a roof of uneven mossy slates. Varying in hue from creamy white to tawny brown, this is the material

that makes up a thousand seductive villages.

Stone is also the predominant building material of the harsher, wilder countrysides of Britain's upland north and west, from the dour, coarse-grained millstone grit of the Pennines to the grey granites of Devon and Cornwall. Hard and difficult to work, particularly in an age before machine tools, these upland rocks were used in rough walls of loosely coursed rubble or moorstone, picked up from the surface of the ground, or in sizeable blocks which give even the smallest cottages a sense of mass, solidity and dignity. Rarely was there any carved detail or refinement, other than a coat of whitewash.

In areas lacking good building stone, people have used what they could find. In some parts of the country there are cottages of sea- or river-rounded cobbles, and the chalk lands of East Anglia, Kent and Sussex have many examples of the ingenious use of flint, usually found in combination with brick or stone.

Once, all cottages would have been thatched – with straw, reed or heather – but the rebuilding of the sixteenth and seventeenth centuries was accompanied by a roofing revolution. Increasingly, thatch was replaced by more durable materials: by stone tiles; by clay pantiles, which came into east coast ports from the Netherlands; and by Welsh and Cornish slate. It survives largely on mud-walled cottages, which are too weak to carry anything else, although many now tiled or slated buildings still have the steep pitch of the original thatched roof, designed for maximum run-off.

Regional differences and vernacular traditions started to break down in the latter half of the eighteenth century, partly because the new canals and better roads made it easier to move materials from one part of the country to another, partly because the publication of builders' pattern books, which soon circulated widely, meant that local craftsmen and estate owners were increasingly aware of the language and practices of fashionable architecture. Increasingly, brick became the preferred material. Although bricks were used in Roman times, brick-making in England only developed in the Middle Ages, and then brick was mostly seen as a base for a facing of stone or flint. Its use began to take off in the fifteenth century, and especially in Tudor times, when many of the great and socially aspiring sought to emulate the brick splendour of Hampton Court. Gradually, like most things, it spread down the social scale, though at first it was used just for chimneys. Early brickwork is attractively varied in colour, ranging from purply red to the softest pink according to the temperature of the kiln and the make-up of the local clay, with some of the most beautiful, of a warm rosy hue, made from the iron-rich Wealden clay. Industrialization brought mass production, and the kind of uniform, strident brickwork that is now seen all over the country.

The self-conscious eighteenth century also saw estate improvement, enclosure, the creation of model villages, and a general flowering of upper-class interest in cottage design. Some concern was purely aesthetic; some economically motivated; some philanthropic. The Georgian fashion for naturalistic landscape parks, in the artfully informal style made popular by Capability Brown, often involved the wholesale removal of a village, and its rebuilding on a new site. In contrast to the settlements they replaced, which had evolved over centuries, these estate villages – the products of a paternalistic, authoritarian landed class – were planned all of a piece. Rigidly laid out, they usually involved cottages of uniform design, generally built in pairs, facing each other across a main street. Accommodation was by no means generous. Two small bedrooms above a main room on the ground floor was a common plan, with a privy out the back, and perhaps a pigsty and woodstore. Various other groups, in particular enlightened industrialists, followed the landowners' lead. Purpose-built communities on greenfield sites were provided with a full range of amenities, the sense of social responsibility which produced them going hand-in-hand with hard-headed business opportunism.

At first, so as not to sully the newly created landscape parks, new villages were built outside the gates, out of sight of the big house. At first, too, while the remodelling of the big house and its surroundings would be entrusted to a fashionable architect or landscape gardener, the new village would be left to a local builder, who usually followed vernacular traditions. In time, attitudes changed. Villages began to be seen as attractions in their own right, not as eyesores, and architects were employed to design all the buildings on an estate, from park lodge to farmhouse. All would conform to a distinctive and consistent style, with wood- and ironwork picked out in paint of the same colour.

Self-conscious prettification reached its ultimate expression in the cult of the Picturesque, a mix of nostalgia and escapism which was fuelled by the ugliness of industrialization and inspired by the pastoral serenity of paintings by such as Claude and Poussin. The isolated cottage in the park was now embellished with decorative bargeboards, leaded lights and a deep thatch, and had ivy and creeper trained up the walls. Inside, it might be a hovel still, but for the well-to-do passer-by these *cottages ornés* summed up all that was desirable about rural life. Often, in a conscious allusion to a destroyed monastic past, they were given gothic windows and other medieval touches. At first, these eye-catchers were intended to be viewed from a distance – from the drawing-room window or from the comfort of a carriage bowling across the park – but in time the rich began building more comfortable versions for themselves, creating country and seaside retreats. And a more scholarly interest in the medieval

past flowered in the careful re-creations of Augustus Welby Pugin, William Burges and other Victorian gothic revivalists.

The vision of the countryside as a world we have lost was given shape, from the early nineteenth century onwards, by a stream of delicate watercolours of rural life by such as Birket Foster, John Linnell and Helen Allingham, while new transport systems, the Victorian landed lifestyle and greater official regulation gave rise to a wealth of isolated cottages, many of them in stunningly beautiful settings, to house a population of lighthouse- and lock-keepers, coastguards, gamekeepers and farm labourers. All were grist to a dream that was quickly picked up by the emergent middle classes, and by artists, writers and others seeking peace and seclusion. Today, as all those joining the traffic streaming out of town on a Friday night testify, the pull of a cottage in the country is as strong as it has ever been.

This exploration of country cottages picks up all these themes. The first section, Local Styles and Materials, looks at vernacular architecture, at the unconscious adaptation of building to place; the second, Estate Architecture and the Picturesque, looks at the designed cottage, and the cottage as romantic eye-catcher; while the third, People and Professions, brings in the cottage as creative retreat, and as the home of those pursuing some of the lonelier, more isolated occupations.

LOCAL STYLES AND
MATERIALS

Whitstone Cottage · Helston
Cornwall

———

THE LONG south-west peninsula that makes up Cornwall, Devon and Somerset has some of the most beautiful landscapes in England, with windswept hills and moors rising above a patchwork of tiny fields and scattered farms and villages, and a dramatic cliffbound coastline. Cornwall, where the underlying rocks never seem far from the surface, is the harsher country, with field walls and buildings of grey stone and slate. Despite the granite boss of Dartmoor, and the heights of Exmoor and its outliers, Devon and Somerset are softer and prettier, their well-watered valleys more fertile, their cottages built of cob, or of the warm red sandstone which colours a swathe of country from Exeter to the Bristol Channel.

Of cob and stone under thatch, this snug eighteenth-century cottage illustrates one of the main strands of the south-west vernacular, although one that is more common in Devon and Somerset than Cornwall. Cob cottages are a kind of human bird's nest, built by paddling together clayey subsoil, water and straw, and then slowly mounding the resulting mixture into walls, with each layer needing to dry before another could be added. Doors and windows were sometimes planned as the walls rose, sometimes cut out afterwards. Built by hand using the most pliable of materials, cob cottages are often endearingly rounded and undulating, and the great thickness of the walls – which are sometimes as much as four feet across – acts as a kind of inbuilt thermostat, keeping interiors warm in winter and cool in summer.

The Birdcage · Port Isaac
Cornwall

———

SLATE IS Cornwall's commonest roofing material, most of it coming from the huge quarry at Delabole which has been worked since at least the sixteenth century and is said to be the largest man-made hole in Britain. Typically, in this part of the world, slates are not only used for roofing but are also hung on upper storeys to protect rough stone walls against the salty air and the driving damp of winter storms.

This bizarre, five-sided eighteenth-century building is a conspicuous feature of the fishing village of Port Isaac, set round a tiny harbour just a couple of miles down the wild north Cornwall coast from Delabole. Steep and narrow alleys – one only twenty inches wide – wind between the cottages and houses stacked up behind the anchorage. Fine Delabole slates were for long shipped out from here, with donkeys used to carry the fragile cargo in panniers down to the quay. The railways took the slate trade, but Port Isaac is still a fishing port, with working boats and lobster pots down by the water and some buildings still arranged in the old way, with living quarters above a windowless lower floor that was used for storing nets.

❧

FERRIS'S COTTAGE · TRELISSICK
Cornwall

———

ON THE gentler south coast of Cornwall, the drowned lower valley of the River Fal runs far inland in a sweep of deep and sheltered water. Overlooking the narrows towards the head of the estuary, where steep wooded slopes close in to either side and the broad river dissolves into a network of branching creeks, is this sturdy nineteenth-century cottage of whitewashed stone and slate. In front, a narrow green canyon of a road leads to the evocatively named King Harry ferry, still the only way, without going miles inland, to the isolated Roseland peninsula which forms the Fal's eastern shore. Just up the hill, a rustic ornamental bridge across the ferry lane gives the clue to Trelissick, the shrub and woodland garden laid out in a sheltered valley above the Fal that is now in the hands of the Trust. Ferris's Cottage is named after one of the gardeners, Mr Ernie Ferris, who lived here for years.

In the garden, views are largely inward, but from some of the higher ground, and from a circular walk through the fringing woods, there are panoramic views of the Fal. A rash of dinghies and excursion craft usually dots the river and, from October to March, there may be some of the sturdy, motorless oyster boats that are unique to the estuary.

Penhaligon's • St Anthony

Cornwall

———

Penhaligon's, built of rough local sandstone under a straw thatch, lies across the water from Ferris's Cottage, on the narrow neck of land curving out to St Anthony's Head, the lighthouse-studded point guarding the eastern approaches to the Fal. This lush and isolated peninsula, with its gentle bays, patches of woodland and quiet farm lanes, is a much softer landscape than that of the harsh north coast, and lays claim to be one of the warmest places in England.

Thatch is now rare in Cornwall, except in some southern parts of the county, but it was once widespread, with the thatcher, slowly working his way up a roof from eaves to ridge, a common sight. Today, straw for thatching has to be specially grown, as modern strains of wheat and other cultivated grasses are too short to make good thatch and are spoilt by combine harvesting. Traditionally, straw for thatching had only the ears harvested; the long stalks were left to be gathered later. Inventive thatchers let their hair down in the patterns created along the ridge, and it was usual to mark the end of a job by perching a corn dolly on the roof.

MORTUARY COTTAGE · LOXHORE
Devon

———

NORTH DEVON is deeply rural, with hamlets and working farms dotted across a rolling wooded landscape of green fields and winding lanes. This sturdy early nineteenth-century cottage is in the tiny settlement of Loxhore Cott, where lanes descend steeply to a bridge across the River Yeo. Built of rendered local sandstone with a slate roof, and originally designed with an all-purpose living room below two atticky bedrooms, the cottage is a good example of the kind of accommodation enjoyed by more fortunate rural labourers in late Georgian times. Many were not so lucky. The first decades of the century, far from bringing the peace and plenty which the end of the Napoleonic wars seemed to promise, were a black period for agricultural workers, with the effects of a general postwar depression aggravated by enclosure and rural overpopulation. Wages fell sharply, and many of the poor were reduced to living in the kind of hovels described by the radical journalist William Cobbett and logged in the reports of various royal commissions, which noted cottages that 'are neither wind nor watertight', with mud floors 'full of vegetable matter', and broken windows stuffed with rags. The lucky ate cheese, butter and milk, but many subsisted on bread, potatoes and water. Despite its deeply rural situation, this cottage was earmarked for use as a mortuary at the start of World War II. No war victims were ever brought here, but the name, Mortuary Cottage, persists.

MORETONHAMPSTEAD
Devon

———

THESE EYE-CATCHING almshouses front a narrow street in the small market town of Moretonhampstead, on the east side of Dartmoor. This is granite country, and here the hard and difficult stone has been shaped into sizeable blocks for the walls, and carved to form the chunky columns for an open eleven-arched arcade fronting the ground floor. Above, under a traditional thatched roof, are long, low, granite-mullioned casements. The boldly carved date-stone over the entrance shows the almshouses were built in 1637, just before the Civil War, but there is no record of who financed them. Unusual both for their time, when granite was rarely worked so carefully for a minor building, and for such a rural backwater, the almshouses are a delightful mixture of the expensive and sophisticated, the unpretentious and local. The classical columns suggest a cultured patron in touch with Renaissance ideas, but the execution is rough and ready, and above the arcade runs a stone drip-mould in the Tudor tradition of the previous century. The whole effect is sturdy and workmanlike rather than refined.

❧

Forge Cottages · Branscombe

Devon

Thatch as a status symbol, and as a mark of affluence rather than poverty, is a feature of the twentieth century. In the Middle Ages almost all buildings, in both town and country, were thatched. Only the most important would have been tiled. In later centuries roof coverings of reed or straw became associated with the humblest dwellings, and with those too poor to afford tiles or slate. Of all roofing materials, though, thatch sits most happily on cottages, always blending in with the countryside around, and ideal for walls too weak to carry the weight of anything heavier.

This delectable pair of cottages is in Branscombe, a south Devon village scattered along a steep-sided combe winding down to the sea. Constructed of plastered stone rubble, they date from the late seventeenth century and were probably built as a row of four tiny one-up, one-downs, with the middle two sharing the central chimney stack, the outer two served by the chimneys on the gable ends. The village forge, which has given the cottages their name, stands nearby and is still working.

Half a mile away, an unstable geological sandwich of clay, chalk and sandstone meets the sea in a spectacular slumped coastline, marked by the grassy ledges of past landslips. South-facing and frost-free, these platforms were once used for raising early vegetables, Branscombe's new potatoes being particularly sought after. The crop was manured with seaweed gathered from the shore and carried up by donkey.

Wychanger Cottage · Luccombe
Somerset

———

SOME OF the most appealing country in the south-west is on the eastern side of Exmoor, where the heather- and bracken-capped hills are broken by the rich Vale of Porlock, running north to the Bristol Channel. Picturesque groups of farms and cottages, many of them dating from the seventeenth century or earlier, dot the valley, with steep wooded slopes running up to open moor behind.

Wychanger Cottage is in Luccombe, a secluded village of cream-washed cob and thatch tucked into a hollow below Exmoor's highest point, the 1,705-foot Dunkery Beacon. The tall chimney, deep thatch eaves and the cottage's uneven, slightly drunken demeanour are all typical of the area, and it has one of the unusual pointed window openings which are a feature of the vale. Behind is the battlemented tower of St Mary's church, which dates from the fourteenth or fifteenth century.

❧

BOSSINGTON

Somerset

———

DOWN THE Vale of Porlock from Luccombe, within smelling distance of the sea, is Bossington, another pretty thatched and cream-washed village. Built of rough local stone rather than cob, this pair of cottages has distinctive round chimney stacks of a kind also found in the Lake District. As in Cumbria, this pragmatic design allowed the builders to use what is basically rubble, unsuited to the kind of precise work needed to create a square stack; larger pieces of stone were rounded on the outer surface to create a curve. The chimney, defiantly placed at a corner of the front wall, is also unusual, reflecting an arrangement which became fashionable in the south-west during the late eighteenth and early nineteenth century.

The wooded slope behind, like all the hillsides around the vale, was originally planted by the Acland family, whose 12,420-acre Holnicote estate embraced all this land. Most active was Thomas Dyke Acland, 10th Baronet (1787–1871), who put in an attractive mix of oak, chestnut, Scots pine and silver fir, and planted a large patch of evergreen oak on the hills above Bossington.

PACKHORSE COTTAGE • ALLERFORD

Somerset

―――

THE WARM red sandstone which underlies much of western Somerset was used for this substantial cottage overlooking the River Aller, about halfway down the Vale of Porlock. Here is another of Somerset's distinctive round chimneys, and the bread oven with its conical roof, like a miniature turret sticking out from the left end of the house, is also a West Country feature. Becoming widespread in the seventeenth century, ovens like this one were often inserted in earlier fireplaces. The pantile roof, replacing the original thatch, is more local. First imported through Bridgwater from the Low Countries in the seventeenth century, pantiles could only be used in places easily reached by water, which meant they were confined in Somerset to areas within spitting distance of the Bristol Channel. A hundred years later pantiles were being made in Bridgwater, but the same transport constraints applied. The serpentine shape of a pantile means it is most suitable for simple roofs, as here, without curves or valleys. In front of the cottage, a cobbled two-arched, packhorse bridge, just wide enough for a laden pony, carries an ancient track across the moors to Minehead, while behind lie steep wooded slopes planted by Thomas Dyke Acland in the 1830s.

ॐ

ARLINGTON ROW · BIBURY

Gloucestershire

SOME OF the most beautiful building stone in England comes from the Cotswolds, where almost every village is constructed of the warm honey-coloured limestone underlying the hills. This enchanting terrace, all irregular gables and moss-encrusted stone, is in the village of Bibury, where the cottages straggle gently uphill away from the River Colne. A short distance upstream, beside the eighteenth-century bridge which carries the main road over the river, is a substantial seventeenth-century fulling mill, a reminder of the wool trade which gave this region its early prosperity and financed so many handsome buildings. The cottages, too, were once connected with the wool trade, having started life in the fourteenth century as a wool store; in the seventeenth century the building was converted to house weavers producing cloth for the mill, and a hundred years later the terrace was extended. Although delightfully individual, Arlington Row illustrates many features of the Cotswold vernacular. The stone, soft and easily cut when first quarried, has been carefully worked to create, among other features, the varied dormers that are so typical of the region, some of them erupting from the roof, others self-important extensions of the main wall. The whole approach, with stone mullions and drip-stones over the windows, is intensely conservative, reflecting the long survival of medieval crafts.

LITTLE BARTLETTS · SOUTH LEIGH
Oxfordshire

———

OLD COTTAGES are often more complex than they look. This delightful pair, known as Little Bartletts after a nineteenth-century owner, stands in the open undulating farmland of the Windrush valley, a couple of miles west of Oxford and in the same limestone belt as the Cotswolds. The ground-hugging, thatch-laden western cottage was originally a small timber-framed medieval house. The owner had a separate sleeping chamber, but all the business of living was done in a hall rising to the rafters, where smoke from an open hearth found its way out through the blackened timbers and thatch which still survive in the roof. In the great rebuilding of the sixteenth and seventeenth centuries, which produced so many exquisite Elizabethan farmhouses, the old timber framing was replaced with local limestone rubble, the hall was floored in, and the open hearth superseded by the massive chimney stack. The stone-tiled, assertive eastern cottage is an eighteenth-century addition, its carefully graded stone roof tiles perhaps coming from the quarry at Stonesfield near Woodstock, about four miles to the north, where farm labourers were hired to dig out the stone in the winter months.

❧

SHERBORNE

Gloucestershire

———

USING WHAT was to hand could mean poaching materials from abandoned buildings. The inhabitants of Avebury in Wiltshire cannibalized the prehistoric stone circle which rings the village; after the dissolution of the monasteries, ruined abbeys and priories were plundered for stone; and this sturdy nineteenth-century cottage incorporates medieval stonework. The striking round-headed doorway with its carved ornament was probably taken from the remains of an abandoned Norman church, and there are some ecclesiastical-looking windows which may have come from the same source. Standing just outside the Gloucestershire village of Sherborne (see also p.86), the cottage is of local limestone rubble, with moss-encrusted stone slates on the roof, and was originally equipped with pigsty and earth closet. At the time it was built, in the mid nineteenth century, stone was still laboriously worked by hand, in what was a highly skilled and labour-intensive industry. A well-dressed stone could take a whole day to prepare; anything fancy very much longer. Traditional skills were passed on from master to apprentice, with medieval practices perpetuated unchanged for centuries. In the later nineteenth century, when it seemed some of the old skills were in danger of dying out, craft techniques were given a boost by the medievalism of the gothic revivalists, spearheaded by the pioneering Augustus Welby Pugin (1812–52).

❧

Thatched Cottage · Mottisfont

Hampshire

———

MANY OLDER structures are buried behind later brick facings. On this west Hampshire cottage, the pleasing brickwork hides a seventeenth-century timber frame, of the same date as the central chimney stack. By the time the facing was put on, in the eighteenth century, the English bond of early brickwork (see p.48) had been superseded by the more economical Flemish bond seen here, with alternate headers and stretchers in each course. The thatch is a regional feature. This part of Hampshire lies at one end of a belt of country, running into Dorset and Somerset, where thatch – and plenty of it – is the rule, giving cottages the soft rounded outlines that are so attractive. On few, though, is thatch used with such abandon as it is here, where it has been brought down in deep wedges between the upper windows and sweeps almost to the ground at one end of the house.

The cottage is in the estate village attached to Mottisfont Abbey, the great house which started life as an Augustinian priory. Close by is the River Test, one of Hampshire's classic trout streams, and for long a focus of village life. In the nineteenth century, water meadows along the river were regularly flooded by a series of ditches connected to the main stream to produce rich crops of hay, and sedge baskets packed with fish would be waiting for the local train each morning.

❧

Rose Cottage · Mottistone
Isle of Wight

———

THIS UNPRETENTIOUS welcoming building with its rose-framed porch lies in Mottistone, a small village clustered round a green on the south side of the Isle of Wight. Close by are the church and ancient manor; the chalk downs rise behind, and there are views over farmland to the sea, less than half a mile away. Dating from late Georgian times, Rose Cottage stands on the cusp of an age, when local traditions and materials were beginning to be affected by nation-wide fashions and practices. The attractively mottled and textured walls, built of a roughly coursed rubble with some huge blocks in among a matrix of smaller pieces, are a mix of the local chalk and greensand, which differs in colour from village to village. But the four-square design, with windows regularly placed and a central door, can be found, with subtle variations, all over England. The classicism which produced the great Georgian country houses is here, however, only skin deep, giving no more than an impression of symmetry and perhaps reflecting the influence of one of the pattern books that now circulated amongst farmers and builders.

CROWN COURT · WEST WYCOMBE
Buckinghamshire
___

T HE FIFTY-MILE arc of the Chilterns running across Oxfordshire and
Buckinghamshire is chalk country. In one of the natural gaps through
the hills, on the old road from London to Oxford, is the village of West
Wycombe, with just a few grander buildings amongst a collection of
timber-framed gabled cottages, several of which date from Tudor times.
Most of the cottages line the main street, but to either side are a couple of
more secluded corners, one of them this quiet grassy court at the east end
of the village. The mix of brick, half-timbering and flint reflects local
materials. Where timber-framing in much of the country is of oak, here
it is likely to be of beech, from the hangers which still cap the Chilterns.
Flint, too, runs with the chalk, in uneven lumpy nodules which have here
been only roughly shaped for building, and there are clay deposits in the
hills for making bricks and tiles.

Nos 32–3, on the left, are among the oldest buildings in West
Wycombe, thought to go back to the fifteenth century. Originally, the
timber-framing was probably infilled with wattle and daub; the attractively
mottled brick nogging, most of it laid in stretcher bond, with courses of
stretchers only, is a later and more durable replacement. Although much
of the brickwork in the village reflects eighteenth-century improvements
by the Dashwood family, whose estate village this was, the infill on these
cottages seems to be earlier.

BRADENHAM
Buckinghamshire

———

EVEN AFTER regional differences started to blur and disappear, local styles and materials continued to be used in self-conscious imitation of the vernacular. In another dip of the Chilterns is the Buckinghamshire village of Bradenham, with picturesque cottages set around a large triangular green. Most of the buildings date back to the sixteenth or seventeenth centuries, with flint and brick facings covering the original timber-framing. These attractive cottages, additions of the mid to late nineteenth century, are both sympathetic to the old village and also atypical. The combination of brick, flint and tile, with the brick quoins and arches giving rigidity and strength to the notoriously difficult flint, is characteristic of the Chilterns, but other details, such as the aggressively latticed windows, and a couple of gothic doorways, are very much of their day.

The layout of the village strongly recalls an age when the lord of the manor was king. Set at the highest point of the green, dominating all, is Bradenham Manor, an arresting red-brick Carolean building which was once the home of Benjamin Disraeli's father, the writer Isaac D'Israeli. The flint village church stands alongside, while the cottages, in ones and twos, straggle down the hill below. Disraeli seems to have had fond memories of the place, and he found an estate for himself at Hughenden, just over the hill.

❧

SAXON COTTAGE · STEYNING

West Sussex

————

SOME COTTAGES are remnants of once grander buildings. Just below the chalk hump of the South Downs, where the River Adur cuts through the hills to the sea, is the small Sussex town of Steyning, where a medieval heyday has left a rich legacy of ancient timber-framed buildings. About half-way down the meandering street that leads up to the Norman church is this perky thatched cottage, with its distinctive cat-slide roof over a weather-boarded extension – an early version of the lean-to – and colour-washed plaster. Although known as Saxon Cottage, it is neither Saxon nor a cottage. Probably built in the 1550s, during the short reign of Mary Tudor, the cottage is the surviving bay of what was once a much larger timber-framed house, set at right-angles to the street. Most likely a building of some importance, it seems to have been provided with a chimney from the start, at a time when this feature was only gradually coming in.

For the first occupants, the 1550s must have been troubled times, with Mary's resolute Catholicism casting long shadows into the furthest corners of her kingdom. On the little green beside the cottage, one John Lauder was burnt at the stake in 1555 for his Protestant beliefs.

South Cottage · Sissinghurst Castle
Kent

————

A CORNER OF the garden at Sissinghurst Castle is the setting for this rose-smothered brick cottage. Like the other buildings and walls forming the skeleton of this legendary Kentish garden, the cottage is a remnant of the great Tudor and Elizabethan house which once stood here, and was originally part of a long wing looking onto a central courtyard. It is a fine example of early brickwork. Although bricks were being made in England in the thirteenth century, they were not at first widely used. But, by the time Sissinghurst Castle was built, with the splendour of Hampton Court and other early Tudor royal palaces as the spur, brick was all the fashion among the great and the socially aspiring. The English bond used here, with alternate courses of headers and stretchers, is typical of the fifteenth and sixteenth centuries. And the bricks would have been locally made, from Wealden clay pressed into wooden moulds and fired in an unreliable, wood-fuelled kiln, which accounts for the attractively varied shades of pink.

When Harold Nicolson and Vita Sackville-West bought Sissinghurst in 1930, South Cottage was where they both slept and he wrote, typing out his books on the desk below the window to the left of the front door. The garden is one of Vita's experiments with concentrated colour, flowering orange, yellow, red and gold in high summer.

☙

LODE LANE · WICKEN FEN

Cambridgeshire

———

For centuries, the East Anglian fens were one of the most impenetrable parts of the country. What is now rich farmland was a watery waste of marsh and mere, home to roving wildfowlers and eel trappers, who lived in hovels built on wooden piles driven into the peat or floated on rafts of compressed reed. All changed in the mid seventeenth century, when the Dutch engineer Cornelius Vermuyden, with the help of a labour force of 11,000 men, started drainage on a grand scale.

This simple, late eighteenth-century cottage in the hamlet known as The Lode stands on the edge of Wicken Fen, one of the few remaining areas of original wetland. Of one storey, as fen dwellings traditionally were, it was built as a two-roomed cottage with a central chimney stack and a ladder to an attic space. Most materials came from the fen. A timber frame, now concealed behind a nineteenth-century brick facing, was probably of imported wood, but there is walling of blocks of sun-dried peat; bundles of reed were used to pack the rough studding and as a base for ceiling plasters; and the thatch is reed, too, with the more flexible grass-like sedge used for the ridge. To the left is a later extension, with a pantiled roof. Within living memory, the remaining fens were still being worked for peat, sedge, reed and buckthorn, and for their harvest of wildfowl, eels and moles, with goods carried out along the ancient waterways known as lodes, after which the hamlet is named.

❧

8 PARK GATES · BLICKLING

Norfolk

———

THE BLICKLING estate, in a loop of the River Bure in north-eastern Norfolk, was something of a backwater for much of the nineteenth century. In Georgian times, the park had been landscaped in fashionable Capability Brown style, but Blickling never had a trigger-happy improving landowner, and as a result, apart from a few Victorian farmhouses and cottages, there is little in the way of estate architecture. Among a number of buildings with a local character is this little cottage, built of plastered mud and thatch. In a region with no good stone but plentiful boulder clay, mud mixed with straw was always an important walling material, and the mud cottages of East Anglia reached heights of sophistication not seen in the West Country. Where Devon and Somerset cob was raised in amorphous layers, the clay-lump of this part of the world was shaped with moulds into rectangular blocks, like American adobe architecture, and then weather-coated with plaster. Today, Norfolk has fewer mud buildings than Suffolk, where the kind of earthy colour-wash seen on this cottage is a common feature of the village scene. An estate valuation of 1756 records numerous mud and thatch cottages at Blickling, but almost all, apart from this survival, have now gone.

❧

WISBECH
Cambridgeshire

———

EAST ANGLIA has been shaped by close contact with Flanders and the Netherlands as much as by its isolation from the rest of the country and lack of good building stone. Flemish immigrants coming into England through east-coast ports in the Middle Ages probably stimulated the practice of building in brick; weavers settling in East Anglia started the fashion for crow-step and curved 'Dutch' gables; and Netherlandish trade financed prosperous merchants' houses in now sleepy country towns.

This garden cottage is attached to one of the most elegant, the Georgian Peckover House, which is part of a long eighteenth-century frontage overlooking the River Nene in the former port of Wisbech. Still lived in by Peckover's head gardener, who now oversees a leafy Victorian layout, the cottage was originally a one-storey building with an atticky upper room lit by a dormer in the roof. Its present form is the result of early twentieth-century alterations. The brickwork of the ground floor, of handmade, eighteenth-century stock, is all in Flemish bond, and gently arched window openings echo those on the main house. The pantiles of the roof, found all along this coast, were originally another Low Countries import; so, too, were the sash windows, which were invented in Holland in the 1680s and introduced to England shortly afterwards.

❧

OLD MILL COTTAGE · BROCKHAMPTON
Herefordshire

———

THIS ISOLATED cottage on the charmingly named Paradise Brook lies deep in a well-wooded Herefordshire valley. Much of the planting here is either nineteenth-century or very recent, but in among the younger trees are some ancient stag-headed oaks, a reminder of the vast forests which once spread across this Welsh border country and provided the raw material for a wealth of delectable timber-framed buildings. One of the most enchanting, the medieval Lower Brockhampton manor, lies just along the valley from the cottage.

The walls of this little building are made of roughly squared local pinkish-grey sandstone, but this is a nineteenth-century facing on what was originally a small cruck-framed house dating back to the fifteenth century. The medieval hall, open to the rafters, was probably floored over in the early seventeenth century, at the same time as the massive stone chimney was built to serve an inglenook fireplace in the main room. Logs and brushwood, available in plenty here, need a large hearth and a flue to match. For long, the cottage was attached to a corn mill on the stream, hence its name.

Tudor Cottage · Styal

Cheshire

———

THE CHESHIRE village of Styal is known as one of the first purpose-built industrial estates. But in among the millworkers' brick terraces (see p.84) are the remnants of a much older agricultural community. This fine cottage, probably originally the house of a prosperous yeoman farmer, is typical of the kind of timber-framed building that characterized the once timber-rich Welsh borders. It is based on a cruck frame, with pairs of massive gently curved timbers supporting the steeply pitched thatched roof, and a separate wood skeleton making up the walls. The spaces between the timbers, now weatherproofed with brick nogging, were probably originally filled with wattle and daub. Originally, too, the cottage may not have looked as black and white as it does now. Although this striking finish is widely seen in the Welsh Borders, it is often a Victorian embellishment to timbers that were originally left to weather to a silvery hue. There is an endearingly belt and braces approach to the roof, with the deep thatch overhangs, designed to throw rain-water clear of the walls, augmented by gutters carried on slender brackets. And the cottage has horizontal sliding windows of the kind known as 'Yorkshire' sashes. Less sophisticated than vertical sashes, these are particularly suited to low-ceilinged rooms with small squat windows.

❧

KINVER EDGE
Staffordshire

———

JUST WEST of the Birmingham conurbation, at the southern tip of Staffordshire, is the prominent sandstone escarpment of Kinver Edge. For centuries, these thickly wooded red cliffs were home to one of the most unusual communities in England, living in cave houses honeycombed deep into the soft and crumbly rock, and making a living by coppicing oak for charcoal and fashioning brooms from twigs of silver birch. Inhabited well into the twentieth century, the rock houses, with their airy, spacious rooms and quarry-tiled floors, were regarded as comfortable and homely, despite the earth closets and the lack of electricity. Niches cut into the walls served as cupboards, and the rock mass itself acted as insulation, keeping houses warm in winter and cool in summer. Each family also had a sheltered garden on the slopes of the Edge. The only problem seems to have been the water that sometimes oozed from the porous rock.

Almost at the top of the escarpment is this terrace of gabled cottages, bizarrely built against – and into – the cliff, with staircases and pantries cut from the solid rock. Abandoned, like the cave houses, for the last thirty years, they have recently been rebuilt by the National Trust, using local sandstone and copying original features.

&

CALKE

Derbyshire

———

ALTHOUGH DERBYSHIRE, one of the Pennine counties, is known for buildings of hard grey stone in bleak upland settings, the southern tip has a softer, more Midlands feel. These cottages, of painted brick and thatch, with delightful eyebrow dormers over the upper windows, lie on the Calke estate, set in the well-wooded agricultural landscape on the border of Derbyshire and Leicestershire. Originally built in the late seventeenth century, they have, like most buildings of any age, been altered and adapted over the years, and turned from one dwelling into two and back again. There are unsympathetic modern windows, but the gabled porches with their scalloped bargeboards are early nineteenth-century additions in the spirit of the Picturesque, perhaps seen as a prettifying touch to a building on the edge of the park, flanking one of the routes to the big house, Calke Abbey. The surrounding village has almost faded away. Once a relatively substantial if scattered settlement of some eighty people, much of it was lost in the late eighteenth century when Calke park was landscaped and greatly enlarged, taking in adjoining farmland. Then, in the 1960s, some outlying buildings disappeared beneath the waters of the new Staunton Harold Reservoir. These cottages are now part of what is little more than a hamlet on a rise overlooking the lake, with a quiet street that leads only to a car park beside the water.

❧

HARDSTOFT
Derbyshire

———

IN THE bleaker landscapes and harsher climates of the north and Wales, stone is king, with field walls, farms and cottages built of rugged, uncompromising limestones and sandstones, of volcanics, or of hard ancient rocks. This terrace, its starkness softened by the cheerfully curtained windows and the border of daffodils and primulas, is in the Derbyshire village of Hardstoft, a former mining community just across the valley – and the roaring M1 – from Hardwick Hall. The cottages are built of roughly shaped and coursed blocks of the local sandstone, which comes from the same geological series as the coal-bearing strata. Although the stone is easily cut when first quarried, the only carefully shaped and finished pieces are the large lintel blocks over doors and windows. The shiny purply-blue roof tiles, obtained from the Stoke-on-Trent area, are also a local feature, characteristic of southern Derbyshire and Staffordshire. Hardstoft was already a coal village in the late seventeenth century, when output here took over from mines within Hardwick park. Half a century earlier, in 1610, the village had been recorded on the estate survey done for Bess of Hardwick's son, William Cavendish, 1st Earl of Devonshire, which shows the villagers' cots and smallholdings arranged along the edge of common land, now long since enclosed.

❦

NEW HOUSE • LANGSTROTHDALE
North Yorkshire

———

THE YORKSHIRE dales are limestone country, with pale grey buildings set in an Arcadian landscape of wide pastoral valleys beneath gently swelling moorland hills. This small late eighteenth-century farm, a two-up, two-down that is more cottage than house, is in Langstrothdale, on the banks of the youthful River Wharfe. Built in an updated version of the classic upland long-house pattern, with one roof embracing both the living quarters and an adjoining byre, it is constructed of the same stone that outcrops in the stream and forms the rugged drystone field wall above the river. Characteristic of the dales are the prominent projecting 'throughs', long stones running across the wall cavity and binding the inner and outer courses together. Also typical are the dressed sandstone blocks forming the lintels and sills of the windows, the low-pitched stone-tiled roof, and the stone cowls on the chimneys.

Much of this upland north country was settled by Norsemen in the ninth and tenth centuries, and it was these hardy pastoralists who gave the English language the regional names for hills, streams and other features of the landscape – among them fell, mere, scar, tarn, beck and crag – which are so evocative of the Yorkshire and Cumbrian scene.

᠂

BIRD HOW • ESKDALE
Cumbria

———

LIKE THE Yorkshire and Northumbria dales, the Lake District on the other side of the Pennines is spectacular hill country, pierced by wide ice-smoothed valleys, and with stone farms and barns that seem rooted in the landscape. This sturdy four-square little building standing alone in a field is gloriously situated towards the head of Eskdale, beneath fells rising to the volcanic crags of Scafell. About a mile upstream, the only road along the valley climbs steeply to Hardknott Pass, guarded by the ruins of a Roman fort. More barn than cottage, Bird How is built of rough blocks of the pink Eskdale granite, gathered from the valley floor and the bed of the river. Local slate covers the roof, with the thick uneven slabs graded in size towards the ridge, and each course weighted down with stones along the gable ends. Now one of the National Trust's holiday cottages, it was built as a small two-storey barn in the distinctive Lake District style, with one side set into a slope and a ramp leading up to the first floor. The underhousing was usually a cattle byre, with hay, oats and barley – the only grains that will grow in the wet Lakeland climate – stored above, but local tradition has it that Bird How was used by shepherds watching over flocks on the fells above.

HIGH HALLGARTH · LITTLE LANGDALE

Cumbria

———

CUMBRIA'S FLAT-BOTTOMED valleys are dotted with long low whitewashed farms, roughly built of field stone and often with an attached byre or barn. This fell cottage, with its front façade covered in a traditional lime-washed render, is built onto a cruck-framed barn, curiously offset from the house. A mongrel of a place, with the seventeenth- or early eighteenth-century core sandwiched between nineteenth-century extensions, High Hallgarth is partly built of stone cleared from the fields (including some massive boulders), and partly of roughly squared quarried blocks. The deep and generous porch, whitewashed inside as well as out, is typically Cumbrian, and there is local slate on the roof. Set on the south side of Little Langdale Tarn, and reached only by an unsurfaced road, the cottage is as remote today as it always was, and still reliant on an earth closet and on water from the gill. The fells which fence in these Lakeland valleys rise all around, with views up the valley to Wrynose Pass, and east towards Ambleside and the softer country around Lake Windermere.

Sarn y Plas

Gwynedd

———

THE SMALL-SCALE landscapes of south-west England, with walled fields below patches of moorland on the hills and a wild coastline, is echoed in Wales's remote, claw-ended Lleyn peninsula, running out into the Irish Sea. Sarn y Plas lies at the far end, in a sheltering patch of trees below the 1,000-foot hump of Mynydd Rhiw. The cottage is typical of the small rugged buildings associated with this part of Wales. With massive walls of local granite, it was built as a simple one-storey dwelling, with part of the ground floor planked over to make a rudimentary second floor, or half-loft, in the roof above, an arrangement known as a crogloft. Reached by ladder, these dark and airless triangles gave storage space and extra sleeping room – for children or servants – without the need for a staircase. Although now tiled, the steep pitch of the roof suggests it was originally thatched, and there are projections on one of the gables for taking ropes to hold the roof down in winter storms. Probably dating from the mid eighteenth century, this was a smallholder's cottage, with a cattle house, or shippon, built up against one end (it is now incorporated in the house). Whitewash is a feature of the Welsh scene, the build-up of material over the years giving older buildings their characteristically ambivalent texture, both smooth and lumpy.

☙

CWMDU
Dyfed

———

THE HEARTLAND of Wales, between Snowdonia and the Pembroke peninsula, is a deeply rural country of scattered farms, where the kind of village found in England, with houses and cottages clustered around a church or green, has never featured. This simple late-Georgian terrace, of colour-washed stone and slate, is a rarity. It is also an echo of a fast vanishing way of life. The main feature of the tiny hamlet of Cwmdu, lying between Carmarthen and Llandovery, the terrace was a community in miniature. Two of the cottagey houses were one-up, one-downs for agricultural workers, but the third is a shop, and a former farmhouse attached to the end of the terrace is an inn. Here, in the informal way found throughout rural Wales, home-brewed beer was tapped directly from a barrel into enamelled jugs and served to customers sitting on settles and benches in the parlour. There was never a bar. A flanking Baptist chapel, founded in 1747, reflects the non-conformist revival which swept through Wales in the eighteenth century. In the wake of the religious fervour stirred up by charismatic Methodist preachers, the land became dotted with chapels. Where the Anglican church stood for alien traditions and the gentry, the often movingly simple buildings of the non-conformists were rooted in Welsh consciousness.

ᘔ

ESTATE ARCHITECTURE AND
—THE PICTURESQUE—

LACOCK
Wiltshire

———

THE ESTATE village is usually seen as an eighteenth- and nineteenth-century phenomenon, associated with the creation of landscape parks and with the workers' communities built by enlightened industrialists, but in fact they go back very much further. This cottage, with the silvery grey timbers of a cruck frame standing out on the end wall, is in Lacock, one of the oldest estate villages in England. Dating from the thirteenth century, the village was built to house those working the lands of Lacock Abbey, founded in 1232 on water meadows by the Avon. Laid out round four streets forming a square, the village is strikingly compact, with gabled cottages – some stone, some timber-framed, and many the result of infilling over the centuries – set on narrow plots running back from the road. Early prosperity was based on the cloth trade, with many houses built with oversailing upper floors to accommodate looms, and on the business generated by a weekly market and annual fair. When the cloth industry declined, Lacock continued to flourish because it lay astride the route from Marlborough to Bristol, which brought a continual stream of travellers to its many inns, but a bypass built in 1745, coupled with a general decline in agriculture, turned it into a backwater. Surviving buildings spanning some five centuries illustrate the seventeenth-century transition from timber to stone, and the Georgian fondness for classical brick façades.

෨

BELTON

Lincolnshire

———

ESTATE ARCHITECTURE as an exercise in philanthropic paternalism also goes back a long way. At Belton, outside the gates of the Brownlow family's four-square Carolean house, is a cluster of cottages and houses in warm local ironstone. Those in a rather heavy-handed Tudor style, with large stone-mullioned windows and massive chimneys, were designed in 1821 by Anthony Salvin, who also gave Belton its village cross.

These unpretentious bedehouses, or almshouses, are among a core of genuine old buildings in the village. Now converted into a pair of dwellings, they were built in 1659 by Lady Alice Brownlow to house six poor elderly women from the estate, as the pious inscription over the arch, *Piae Genectae Domus* (the house of good people), suggests. Built of local stone, with a nineteenth-century slate roof, and planned round a courtyard in the medieval manner, with each resident given a living-room and kitchen to themselves, the almshouses are typical of the kind of minor charitable foundation with which the wealthy up and down the country eased their consciences. Certainly, 'Old' Sir John and Lady Alice did not lack for funds or for generosity. Childless themselves, they took to giving nephews, nieces and other members of the family gifts of money from the sacks of coin which they had hidden around the house.

இ

Woolley Lodge · Arlington

Devon

————

THIS LITTLE tree-framed bungalow set behind wrought-iron gates on the scenic road from Barnstaple to Lynton is a piece of late Georgian estate architecture. Designed as a lodge for Arlington Court, the former seat of the Chichester family, it was built in the early 1820s at the same time as the plain classical villa across the park, on the other side of the deep wooded valley of the River Yeo. The architect was Thomas Lee (1794–1834), a local man from Barnstaple, whose training in the London office of the distinguished John Soane (1753–1837) perhaps accounts for the lodge's severe boxy lines and temple-like aspect, which give faint echoes of Soane's design for Dulwich Art Gallery. Lived in by the gardener rather than a gate-keeper, the lodge guarded a drive which was rarely used. If Sir John Chichester, the son of Arlington's builder, had had his way, however, this single-storey cottage would have marked the start of a triumphal approach to the house. Sir John planned a drive which would zig-zag down through the woods along the Yeo, crossing the lake he had created on the river by a grandiose suspension bridge. His death put an end to the scheme, but the vegetation-encrusted piers of the bridge (all that was completed) still stand in the valley.

Oak Cottages • Styal
Cheshire
———

THESE PRETTY brick and slate cottages, with colourful gardens across a narrow cobbled lane, hardly fit the stereotyped view of industrial housing. But this is what they are. Part of the Cheshire village of Styal, they represent one of the first purpose-built industrial communities, developed by the Georgian entrepreneur Samuel Greg to house the workers for his new cotton mill. The massive water-powered mill, set deep in the leafy valley of the River Bollin, was built by 1784; the village, spaciously laid out amongst fields some distance away, grew slowly over several decades, as the business expanded. Oak Cottages, shown here, are additions of the 1820s, and were not such a major advance on their urban counterparts as they might look. Basically two-up, two-downs, each with its privy in a yard behind, the cottages housed families of up to fourteen. The unique feature was that each was also provided with a substantial allotment. These early factory colonies were treated as a variant of the model estate village, designed all of a piece and with a range of facilities. Greg provided his workers with a shop, bakehouse, school and, echoing his own beliefs, non-conformist chapel. Built of local red brick, and with an overall sense of the Georgian intuition for proportion and design, everything is both pleasing and functional.

❧

SHERBORNE

Gloucestershire

———

THESE PRETTY limestone cottages are part of a nineteenth-century model village on the former estate of the Lords Sherborne in Gloucestershire. On the other side of the park and the big house from a remnant of the old village, with its traditional Cotswold cottages, these buildings were designed in conscious imitation of the local vernacular, with gabled dormers and carved drip moulds over stone-mullioned windows. The symmetrical façades and the size and shape of the windows give the game away, and the nineteenth-century development as a whole, with cottage pairs and terraces strung out along the main street, is too ordered and uniform to be anything but purpose-built. All the cottages are south-facing, all are set back behind front gardens, and all have substantial limestone walls on to the road. When built, each was provided with a pigsty for the animal which was every cottager's pride and joy. Flora Thompson's nostalgic evocation of country life at the turn of the century, *Lark Rise to Candleford*, describes the children being sent to glean the hedgerows for choice long grass and snails for piggy's supper, the Sunday callers who came to see the pig, not the family, and the feast of pork and bacon which followed the yearly killing.

&.

YSBYTY IFAN

Gwynedd

———

IN THE mid nineteenth century, Colonel Douglas-Pennant, later 1st Baron Penrhyn, set about enlarging and improving the Snowdonia estate attached to his grandiose family seat – a neo-Norman castle by Thomas Hopper – on the north coast of Wales. Tenants were treated to an address, printed in both English and Welsh, criticizing their husbandry, and old farmhouses and other buildings were extensively renewed.

The remote village of Ysbyty Ifan, set in the rugged hill and valley country south of Betws-y-Coed, was bought by Douglas-Pennant in 1854, together with 25,000 acres of shooting country (see p.138). Strung out along the alder- and willow-lined banks of the River Conwy, the little community was almost entirely rebuilt in a vernacular revival style, with rows of slate-roofed rough stone cottages, a new school, parsonage and drinking fountain, and new almshouses to replace an originally seventeenth-century foundation. The parish church, completed in 1861, is on the site of the twelfth-century hospice which gave its name to the place (Ysbyty Ifan means the hospital of St John). Offering a refuge in a wild and lawless land, the village prospered from being on the old road through the mountains to Caernarfon and Anglesey. Telford's new road, built in the 1820s and followed by the present A5, took away the traffic, and only a few remnants of the old village survive, among them a fine double-arched eighteenth-century bridge across the Conwy.

ॐ

Boycott Pavilions · Stowe

Buckinghamshire

THE EIGHTEENTH-CENTURY interest in landscaping led to the building as ornament, with countless temples, obelisks, triumphal arches and other eye-catchers artfully placed to focus a view across a park. This baroque pavilion, essentially a cottage disguised as an architectural fancy, and primarily intended to be looked at, is a feature of one of the earliest and greatest of these Georgian landscapes. Covering some four hundred acres of Buckinghamshire, Stowe landscape garden was created by three generations of the high-flying Temple-Grenville family, with the help of an impressive company of native and continental talent. The pavilion, designed *c.*1728 by James Gibbs, is part of the early development of the garden, and is one of two built as lodges to mark the southern entrance to the park. Originally they were topped off with pyramids. When the garden was extended, they became incidents on the approach to the house, and the pyramids, which were now thought too angular, were replaced by domes. At first, too, only one – built as a retirement home for an old soldier – could be lived in. Richard Temple, Viscount Cobham, who started the garden layout, had played a major part in the Duke of Marlborough's campaigns against the French in the early years of the century, and had one pavilion fitted out for a veteran of the wars, Major Sam Speed. The other was turned into a house much more recently.

THE GOTHIC COTTAGE • STOURHEAD
Wiltshire

———

THE SERENE eighteenth-century landscape at Stourhead, with classical temples set round a lake and wooded slopes rising from the water, includes this distinctly unclassical building amongst the greenery on the western shore. A one-roomed gothic cottage of local rubble and limestone with a roughly tiled roof and creeper coating, its main feature is this splendid stone bay, with traceried windows and an elaborately carved exterior bench. Probably dating originally from the mid eighteenth century, when the garden was laid out by Henry Hoare II, the cottage was given its present Picturesque appearance by Richard Colt Hoare, Henry's grandson, who inherited Stourhead in 1785. Henry's favourite grandchild and a frequent visitor to Stourhead in his early years, when he would have been able to watch some of the temples going up, Sir Richard generally respected his grandfather's creation, confining his embellishments to laying down some gravel paths, adding some exotic trees and, in 1806, altering an existing garden feature into this romantic fantasy. As well as the window bay, he devised a gothic porch with pointed openings, and a planked front door with long strap hinges. The gothic cottage is just the kind of rustic eye-catcher that the upper classes were busy adding to their estates in the late eighteenth and early nineteenth centuries, in line with the vogue for the Picturesque. It may once have been lived in, but it has been a summerhouse since at least 1895.

ॐ

The Convent in the Wood

Wiltshire

———

THIS IS the cottage as theatre. Buried deep in a Wiltshire wood, this heart-warming fantasy, built between 1760 and 1770, was designed to be visited by carriage from the main house, over a mile away. The accommodation, with two bedrooms above a drawing-room and dining-hall, is actually relatively generous; legend has it that guests who fell sick at the big house were secreted here until they recovered. Known as the Convent in the Wood, it is a kind of ecclesiastical dacha, with a belfry in one of the turrets, suitably churchy windows, and rustic façades – the masonry equivalent of bark-covered timbers and twiggy fencing – created by facing brick walls with random lumps of apparently mortarless limestone and flint. Originally, it boasted glass from Glastonbury Abbey, and an interior which included painted panels showing nuns in the dress of the various different orders. This is the Picturesque at its most extreme, with all the components of the style – irregularity, thatch, gothic details and plenty of texture – brought together in a glorious piece of make-believe. The effect is all. Not surprisingly, although cottages such as this enhanced the view and the reputation of their builder, they were hardly economic, proving both expensive to construct and costly to maintain.

ã

ORCHARD COTTAGE · NEWHOUSES
Cornwall

———

THE CHEAPEST way to produce a Picturesque cottage was to dress up an existing building. Devon is divided from Cornwall by the deep wooded valley of the Tamar, looping and winding its way to the sea at Plymouth. A few miles upstream, on the Cornish side of the river, is the National Trust's Cotehele estate, where Orchard Cottage, its striking frontage half hidden by greenery, stands beside a back drive to the house. The round-headed windows with their latticed gothic panes and the quaint stable door suggest a purpose-built rural retreat, but this façade is only skin-deep. Originally a modest early nineteenth-century building attached to a smallholding, with its former cowhouse – now converted into another cottage – behind, Orchard Cottage was later prettified in the spirit of the Picturesque, to make a decorative eye-catcher beside the drive.

Used by the Edgcumbe family only as a carriage route to St Dominick church, about half a mile away, this drive is particularly associated with the formidable Lady Ernestine, who lived at Cotehele for some twenty years at the turn of the century. A supporter of the temperance movement, and probably responsible for closing various pubs round about, Lady Ernestine believed in keeping up appearances. Every Sunday she would be driven to church by a coachman in full livery, attended by cockaded footmen.

DOYDEN CASTLE · PORT QUIN

Cornwall

———

PERCHED ON the twin-humped headland sheltering the south side of
Port Quin (see p.120) is a castellated stone folly known as Doyden
Castle. More cottage than castle, its few rooms stacked one above the
other, Doyden Castle was built *c.*1830 by the wealthy Wadebridge rake
Samuel Symons as a retreat for drinking and gambling (his capacious wine
bins are a feature of the ground floor). With its pinnacled angle buttresses,
pointed windows and battlements, Doyden Castle is a wonderfully situated
example of the romantic cottages and other fantasies, some of them
purpose-built ruins, with which the landed gentry of the late eighteenth
and nineteenth centuries adorned their parks and estates. Although Samuel
Symons Esq planned Doyden Castle as a place to entertain his cronies, it is
possible it doubled up as an eye-catcher, designed to be seen silhouetted
against the sky, with the sea appearing like lakes between the humps of the
headland. On the cliffs nearby are the fenced-off shafts of an abandoned
antimony mine, whose ore would once have been shipped out from
Port Quin.

BLAISE HAMLET

Avon

———

By the end of the eighteenth century there were isolated romantic cottages dotted up and down the country, but the first Picturesque village, Blaise Hamlet, was not built until 1810–12. Commissioned by the philanthropic Quaker banker John Scandrett Harford, to house his aged retainers, Blaise was designed by the versatile John Nash (1752–1835), whose adaptable talents were shortly to be exercised on Brighton Pavilion. The hamlet is the ultimate in studied informality and self-conscious use of the vernacular. The nine cottages are loosely grouped round an undulating close-cropped green, with a tall pump-cum-sundial, carelessly off-centre, as a suitably arresting focal point. Although all – as in a model village – are to the same scale, no two buildings share a common design. Some are tiled, others thatched (with the deepest of overhangs), some are all curves, others have sharp edges, two incorporate dovecotes, others are supplied with a shady verandah. Most striking are the cottages' monstrous brick chimneys, designed to be seen silhouetted against trees behind. Blaise is much closer to a stage-set than the real thing, with a sense of exaggeration about the detailing. Even the local rubble used for the walls has not been treated in the traditional way, with the biggest stones at the bottom, but has been randomly laid, to give a rugged effect. And the names – Sweetbriar Cottage, Rose Cottage – are those of a head-in-the-clouds romantic.

ATCHAM

Shropshire

———

SEVERAL YEARS before Blaise Hamlet (see p.100), Nash had been engaged by Thomas Hill, 2nd Lord Berwick, to alter some cottages in the village of Atcham, at the gates of Attingham Park. Nash first came to the Shropshire estate in the late 1790s as junior partner to the celebrated Humphry Repton, who had been commissioned to landscape the park, and he had been largely responsible for carrying out Repton's proposals. By the time the cottages were worked over, *c.*1802, the two men had parted company. One of the most versatile and inventive of nineteenth-century architects, Nash made use of every conceivable style, with much of his enormous output, such as his stuccoed London terraces, planned on a grandiose scale. This pretty colour-washed building is restrained and small-scale but its playful window bay, the kind of light-hearted gothic detailing that was distinguished from the real thing, and from the work of Victorian medievalists, by being spelt gothick, is firmly in the spirit of the Picturesque.

Nearby is an example of another side of Nash's work. Set amongst fields beyond the village, across the River Severn, is his more ambitious Cronkhill, an Italianate villa with a round corner tower, arched windows and Roman-style colonnade.

৵

Bow Cottage · Selworthy

Somerset

———

SIR THOMAS DYKE ACLAND, who transformed the landscape of the Vale of Porlock (see p.28), was captivated by the vernacular buildings of the area and in 1828 re-created the village of Selworthy in a self-consciously rustic idiom. This cream-washed thatched cottage, like a more flamboyant version of those found in Luccombe, Allerford and elsewhere, is one of seven loosely grouped around a sloping green at the foot of a steep wooded combe climbing to Selworthy Beacon. All in the same spirit but each subtly different, the cottages were designed by the baronet to incorporate almost every feature of the local vernacular, from the tall chimneys – some of them rounded – and projecting ovens to the deep thatch eaves and eyebrow dormers, and were also given some Picturesque features of his own. At the top of the village is the fifteenth-century church of All Saints, its limewashed walls and battlemented tower standing out conspicuously in views across the valley.

In re-creating Selworthy, Sir Thomas was probably encouraged by his friend John Harford, who had commissioned John Nash to design Blaise Hamlet some eighteen years earlier (see p.100). Both men were inspired by social concern and the cult of the Picturesque, but their creations – though both were intended to be some kind of rural idyll for retired estate workers – are quite different. Acland's is the less showy and self-conscious; none the less, he provided his pensioners with red cloaks for Sundays, when they were expected to congregate beneath the walnut trees on the green.

❧

Chapel Cottage · Oxburgh
Norfolk

———

DEEPENING INTEREST in the medieval in Victorian times led to the self-conscious enhancement of some genuine old buildings. Among them was Oxburgh Hall, a moated brick manor house in the Norfolk fen country, where extensive alterations, such as the addition of twisting terracotta chimneys and oriel windows, made an already striking house even more eventful. This little brick cottage is in the grounds, built up against the park wall. Originally seventeenth-century, it was given its present gothic veneer, with leaded casements, elaborate bargeboards and the illusion of ornate timber-framing painted on the end wall, towards the end of the nineteenth century. Like the chapel nearby, built several years before the cottage was remodelled, all is in the spirit of the hall, but the cottage still retains strong links with the local vernacular. Norfolk cottages were typically of one and a half storeys, with dormers lighting the upper rooms; roofs in this part of the world are usually pantiled (the black glazing seen here is a local variant on the more usual red); and crow-stepped gables, like the original one at the far end, were one of the features introduced to East Anglia from Holland. Another Dutch device is the 'tumbling in' used on the seventeenth-century gable, where wedges of bricks are laid at right angles to the slope of the roof.

CHURCH COTTAGE · STUDLEY ROYAL
North Yorkshire

———

ONE OF the nineteenth century's arch-medievalists was the architect William Burges (1827–81), who was commissioned by George Robinson, 1st Marquess of Ripon, to build a church on his Yorkshire estate. With its soaring spire crowning a rise in the deer park, and a richly decorated interior, the church is part eye-catcher, part symbol of the Marquess's fervent Anglo-Catholicism. This eclectic building, designed to house the church organist (the Marquess was passionate about organ music), stands just east of St Mary's, looking onto the long lime avenue running up from the park gates. Built in the 1870s, at the same time as the church, and more house than cottage, it uses a wealth of gothic detail, all of it in Burges's usual heavy-handed style. The roof line is gabled and dormered, with a large gargoyle incorporated in one of the copings and a finialled tower derived from a French château at one corner; mullioned windows are topped off with blank trefoil heads; a short arcade shelters a stone bench; and there are leaded lights, carved heraldic shields and the stag – here looking more like Bambi – of the Marquess's badge. Some timber-framing is an incongruous nod to rural traditions in other parts of the country, but the facings and dressings are of local gritstone, with some of the stones laid to rise through two courses in the technique known in this part of England as 'snecking'.

The Lodge • Hardcastle Crags

West Yorkshire

———

VICTORIAN GOTHIC comes in almost every shape and form. This mid nineteenth-century lodge in glorious country just west of Yorkshire's textile towns marks the entrance to the deep wooded valley of the Hebden Water, which tumbles off bleak Pennine moorland a couple of miles to the north. The great attraction, which has brought tourists here since Victorian and Edwardian times, is the dramatic outcrop of millstone grit, known as Hardcastle Crags, on the north side of the valley, and it is quarry-dressed gritstone of which the lodge is built. Also local are the oversized sandstone quoins at each corner of the building, but there are red clay tiles rather than local stone flags on the roof. The lodge was built for the Savile family as an eye-catcher at the start of a picturesque carriage drive leading up to their shooting box at the head of the dale, with gothic details enlivening what is basically a T-shaped bungalow. There are mullioned windows, one of them surmounted by a Tudor-style sandstone drip mould, but most of the interest is focused on the canopied porch set in the angle between the north and east wings. The oversized bargeboard on the gable end is pierced with medieval quatrefoils and trefoils, there are wooden bosses carved with oak leaves, and the entrance door has been made to a medieval pattern, with exaggerated iron strap hinges.

SEVEN GABLES COTTAGE · CLIVEDEN

Buckinghamshire

———

JEROME K. JEROME, creator of *Three Men in a Boat*, thought the great loop of the Thames upstream of Maidenhead, where the wooded slopes of Cliveden rise steeply from the water, one of the sweetest stretches on the river. Seven Gables Cottage sits on the north bank, at the foot of the Cliveden woods, where a drive through the grounds comes sweeping down to a boathouse on the river. Dating from 1857, it was built only a few years after the Italianate palace on the hill, but there is no comparison in style. Whereas the house was the creation of Sir Charles Barry, this substantial eye-catcher, and another similar on the other side of the boathouse, were the work of George Devey (1820–86), and are early examples of the 'Wealden' style that became his trademark. The mix of brick and half-timbering, the jettied upper floor carried on conspicuous brackets, the red roof tiles and the tall ornamental chimneys are all borrowed from the vernacular architecture of the Kent and Sussex Weald, though re-interpreted in an individual idiom. Devey was later to work extensively for the Rothschilds on their estates in the Vale of Aylesbury, creating an overgrown Tudor cottage at Ascott and leaving a rich legacy of stables, lodges and other minor buildings. His approach, based on old methods and materials, was later taken up by Norman Shaw, W. E. Nesfield and Arts and Crafts architects.

❧

COLETON FISHACRE

Devon

———

ABOUT HALF-WAY along the unspoiled stretch of south Devon coast between Kingswear and Brixham, the cliffs are broken by a secluded valley where a leafy garden runs steeply uphill to the seductive country house built here in 1925–6. Designed by Oswald Milne (1881–1968), a pupil of Edwin Lutyens, the house is an unpretentious, almost cottagey building in the Arts and Crafts tradition, built of local stone quarried from the combe, and with a long steeply pitched roof, prominent chimneys and small-paned casement windows.

There is no hint of grandeur, but the latest conveniences were not forgotten. Tucked away behind the house are these quarters for the chauffeur, with first-floor accommodation over a purpose-built garage area, complete with awning (and, when first built, petrol pumps). The design of this service building echoes that of the house, with Delabole slates (see p.14) covering the steeply pitched roof, but the walls, of rubble stone from the garden quarry, have been roughly plastered rather than left bare. Milne was working for Rupert and Lady Dorothy d'Oyly Carte, beneficiaries of the family interest in Gilbert and Sullivan's comic operas; they are said to have spotted the valley from the sea, when cruising along the coast in their yacht.

BIDDULPH GRANGE
Staffordshire

———

THIS APPROXIMATION to a Cheshire cottage, with its decorative bargeboards and fake half-timbering, is a High Victorian version of the Georgian eye-catcher. Built in 1856, as the date on the gable proclaims, it is a feature of the unique Staffordshire garden created by James Bateman, whose initials are intertwined with those of his wife Maria above the first-floor window. Grandson of a wealthy Black Country industrialist, Bateman used much of his inherited fortune to turn a stretch of inhospitable moor into the most eccentric and theatrical of garden layouts. Apart from the stone pine cones on the parapet walls to either side, a reference to the exotic conifers all around, the cottage seems straightforward enough. But this half-timbered façade with its sandstone chimney sits back-to-back with a stone and topiary re-creation of an Egyptian temple, with sculpted sphinxes guarding walls, obelisks and a pyramid of clipped yew. And those who venture inside the cottage will be confronted with a statue of a squat and ugly ape-like Egyptian deity, chosen by Bateman because he was an attendant of the god Thoth, who was associated with botany.

PEOPLE AND PROFESSIONS

LACOMBE • PORT QUIN
Cornwall

THIS STURDY fisherman's cottage, of whitewashed stone rubble with a slate roof, stands in a huddle of buildings around a tiny harbour on Cornwall's rugged north coast, where the sea has etched out a fault line in the rock. Once a community of almost a hundred, Port Quin is now a shadow of its nineteenth-century self, when coastal vessels came into the shallow inlet on a rising tide to load antimony and lead from local mines, and when a lookout was stationed on the cliffs above to watch for the shoals of pilchards that were once a mainstay of the Cornish economy. There are no fishermen here now, but immediately in front of this cottage is the substantial shed-like cellar or 'palace' where the catch was taken to be salted down and pressed into barrels; the fishy waste was used to manure the fields round about. Local legends tell of the men of the village being lost at sea in an overwhelming disaster, but it is more likely that the community faded away after a series of poor fishing seasons and the failure of the mines, with some of the villagers perhaps emigrating to Canada.

FOREST COTTAGES · KILLERTON
Devon

———

THE APTLY named Forest Cottages sit in a small clearing in the middle of Ashclyst Forest, a 600-acre mosaic of oak, beech, larch and pine. The forest – some of it ancient woodland, some of it dating from early nineteenth-century plantings – marks a patch of high infertile land in the rich Devon farming country north-east of Exeter. The improver was Sir Thomas Dyke Acland of nearby Killerton House, who is better known for transforming his Holnicote estate (see p.28). Sir Thomas developed the forest as a source of building timber, using teams of horses to haul out the felled trunks, and as a place to raise pheasants and other game. Of the six gamekeepers he employed, two lived in these isolated cottages, fencing them round with the strung-up corpses of crows, weasels and other vermin. Despite the tiled brick extension at one end, the cottages go back to the eighteenth century, and are traditionally built, with walls of local stone rendered against the weather. The steeply pitched, straw-thatched roof is a common sight in this part of the country, with many more decorative examples, but there is something pleasing about Forest Cottages' eyebrow dormers, hooped high over the bedroom casements. Today, the woods are threaded with public paths and are still home to a rich variety of wildlife, with the sunny glades attracting some thirty species of butterfly.

❧

BUSCOT
Oxfordshire

SOME TWO hundred miles from the North Sea, where Oxfordshire runs into Gloucestershire and Wiltshire, just above the attractive town of Lechlade, the Thames ceases to be navigable. The last lock before Lechlade is at Buscot, where this quaint keeper's house sits on an island in the river, overlooking the weir pool. The square two-storey main block dates from *c.*1790, when Edward Townsend Loveden, owner of the Buscot estate, headed a commission to improve navigation on the Upper Thames. The year before, the final section of a linking canal to the Severn had been opened, joining the Thames a few miles west of Buscot, and something had to be done to ease the flow of traffic on this stretch of the river. Unlike most lock-keepers' cottages, though, this one was built by the astute Loveden to serve two purposes. As well as collecting tolls from passing barges, the keeper was also in charge of three deep fish tanks constructed beneath a lean-to on the north side of the house. Connected to the river by an underground channel, and safe from poachers, these tanks gave a constant supply of fresh fish for the big house which Loveden had built on the south bank of the Thames some ten years before.

In time, the railways killed the river traffic, and the canal link to the Severn is no longer open.

KNOWLES FARM COTTAGE · ST CATHERINE'S
Isle of Wight

————

THIS FARM cottage stands on the windswept southern tip of the Isle of Wight, close to the lighthouse marking St Catherine's Point. The belt of greensand which runs down the south side of the island is here overlain by slippery blue clay, and land meets sea in an unstable, slumped cliff-line extending some six miles along the coast, the largest region of coastal landslip in northern Europe. Much of the distinctively terraced undercliff was formed by movements thousands of years ago, but not far from the cottage is a wild and tumbled heath which resulted from a couple of cataclysmic landslides in the summer of 1928, the second of which carried away the old coast road.

Built for workers on Knowles Farm, which runs down to the foreshore here, the cottage is a simple whitewashed building of stone and slate, with atticky bedrooms lit by the dormer windows that break the roof line. Stone-walled fields, the only ones found on the island, criss-cross the country around. Farming has always been difficult, dependent on the grazing of sheep on the island's chalk downs, and traditionally supplemented by fishing and smuggling. This is fine bird-watching country, with many species attracted to the varied flora in the sheltered hollows of the undercliff, and migratory birds congregating at the point in late summer.

OLD WEIR COTTAGE · SWAINSHILL
Herefordshire

———

THE 1850s and 60s saw the high summer of Victorian farming, between the slump which followed the end of the Napoleonic wars and the deep depression at the end of the century, caused by a flood of cheap grain and meat from America and Australia and a run of poor summers. Mechanization came in only slowly, with the number of farm workers reaching a peak in 1851 and traditional methods, such as threshing with a flail, continuing into the twentieth century.

These functional cottages, their starkness softened by the gently arched windows and doors and by the green fields of the pastoral Wye valley, are typical of the kind of no-frills accommodation built for estate workers during the Victorian golden years. Basic two-up, two-downs of orangey-red brick and slate, they reflect a concept that is urban rather than rural, like a fragment of the city set down in the countryside. Although now converted into one dwelling, they still have most of their original features, with brick-built coppers with cast-iron tubs in the lean-tos at each end, and late nineteenth-century ranges in the kitchens. The Victorian brickwork seems to have been done with an eye to economy: while the front is built of Flemish bond, the side walls are more irregular, with some courses consisting of stretchers alone.

BIRLING GAP
East Sussex

'FIVE AND twenty ponies; Trotting through the dark; Brandy for the Parson; 'Baccy for the Clerk....' With its many estuaries, creeks and coves, and a total length of some 6,000 miles, the British coast seems tailor-made for smugglers. The brandy and tobacco of the Napoleonic wars, which Kipling refers to in his poem, is now more likely to be narcotics and illegal immigrants, but small boats coming into shore under the cover of darkness are still used by those wanting to avoid inquiring eyes.

This terrace of workmanlike coastguard cottages was built in 1850 for men patrolling one of the most beautiful stretches of the south coast, where the South Downs meet the sea in the chalky turf-thatched humps known as the Seven Sisters. Starkly built of rendered concrete and grey slate, and set end-on to the sea in an uncompromising line, the cottages have no links with the vernacular architecture of south-east Sussex, but in a strange way their unloveliness points up the natural beauty of this fragile coast. The distinctive switchback outline of the Sisters is the result of steady erosion of a ridge and valley landscape, and the cliffs continue to recede year by year. At least one cottage has been lost to the sea, another is teetering on the brink, and eventually the whole terrace will go over the cliff.

DUNWICH HEATH
Suffolk

———

THIS FUNCTIONAL brick and slate terrace rising from a sea of gorse on the Suffolk brecklands was built in the 1860s for coastguards policing one of the loneliest stretches of coast in England. Now gleaming white, the cottages were originally weather-proofed with tar. And the look-out tower at one end, with a strip window giving 270 degree vision up and down the coast, was given its present form in World War II, when the terrace became a link in Britain's sea defences and a radar station was based in one of the cottages.

Like the chalk cliffs of Sussex (see p.130), this is a fragile landscape, where East Anglia's sands and gravels reach the sea in a low, crumbling cliff line backed by marsh and heath. Once, these coastal heaths were locked into the local economy, used for grazing the great flocks of sheep which underlay Suffolk's medieval prosperity; and not far to the north is the straggle of houses and tumbled stone which is all that remains of the once flourishing cathedral city of Dunwich, Saxon capital of East Anglia, which was gradually overwhelmed by the sea. Every year, winter storms further erode the cliffs.

Brownsea Island

Dorset

THIS INTRIGUING gothick terrace is on the eastern tip of Brownsea Island, overlooking the narrow waterway leading into Poole Harbour. Dating from the early nineteenth century, and constructed of rendered brick, it was built for men of the coastguard service, with a more grandiose residence for their commanding officer set just along the shore. A coastguard service, backed up by ten-gun batteries, started operating from Brownsea in the eighteenth century, both as an attempt to protect shipping from privateers and as a check on rampant smuggling. In earlier days the island itself had been a centre for illicit trade, used for storing cargoes of raisins, almonds, herrings and Brazil wood.

This tiny shoreside settlement, embellished with castellations, crowstep gables, armorial shields and even a couple of arrow slits, is all of a piece. Out of the picture is the toytown Brownsea Castle, which started life as one of Henry VIII's blockhouses defending the south coast against the French. After a fire in 1897, it was rebuilt as an unbuttoned late Victorian extravaganza, and has a landing stage to match, complete with octagonal battlemented turrets and marble steps. During Brownsea's Edwardian heyday, a stream of minor royalty alighted here, but today the island is best known as one of the last southern haunts of the red squirrel.

SOUTER LIGHTHOUSE
Tyne and Wear

———

SOME COTTAGES in spectacular coastal locations were built for those tending one of the many lighthouses that were renewed or constructed in Victorian times. This purposeful nineteenth-century terrace, cheek by jowl with the rocket-like lighthouse tower and providing accommodation for six families in all, is on the Northumbrian coast, on the headland overlooking the southern approaches to the Tyne. Built in 1870, the 76-foot-high lighthouse was the first to be powered by an alternating electric current, and could be seen from some nineteen miles out to sea. The whole lighthouse complex overlooks one of the few unspoilt stretches of this heavily industrialized coast, where the limestone cliffs are eroded into caves, stacks and rock arches. Ledges and shelves in the cliffs attract huge numbers of seabirds. Migrant snow bunting can be seen in winter, but for bird-watchers the big draw is Marsden Rock, an impressive offshore stack pierced by a natural arch, which supports a large colony of breeding kittiwakes.

TŶ CIPAR

Gwynedd

———

SET ON a vast heather moorland on the eastern side of Snowdonia, with Llyn Conwy, source of the Conwy river, just a short walk away, this sturdy building of local stone and slate was originally a gamekeeper's cottage. Known as Tŷ Cipar, it was one of several on the extensive sporting estate acquired by the future 1st Lord Penrhyn, of Penrhyn Castle, in the mid nineteenth century. Shooting parties were housed in a couple of villas down the Conwy valley. To preserve proprieties, young ladies and married couples stayed at one, young men at the other, with a pony and trap provided to bring the two parties together after a sustaining breakfast. The 2nd Lord Penrhyn was as keen a sportsman as his father, dividing his time between his racehorses, which won numerous trophies, and his birds; *Bailey's Monthly Magazine of Sports and Pastimes* reported in 1888 that: 'The 12th [of August] finds him on his Welsh moors, whence nothing can lure him till the saddling bell at Doncaster sends forth its Leger clang.' During the Indian summer of Edwardian days, some 500 brace of grouse and 3,000 pheasant were reared annually on the Snowdonia estate, but the number of birds shot declined rapidly after World War I, which claimed the 3rd Lord's elder son and his two half brothers.

MONK'S HOUSE · RODMELL

East Sussex

———

THIS IS the cottage where Virginia and Leonard Woolf lived from 1919 until their deaths. Set in the quiet Sussex village of Rodmell, between the South Downs and the Ouse, it looks on to a winding lane falling steeply to the river. At the back, there are wide views to the downs, with a tiny flint church set like an eye-catcher just over the garden wall. Virginia loved the place and its isolation, discouraging an over-eager visitor with itemized disadvantages – 'view is ruined'; 'smallest doghole for you'; 'village char is cook' – and retiring to a shed in the garden to write.

One of the older buildings in the village, Monk's House dates back to the sixteenth century, but its originally timber-framed walls were largely rebuilt in the seventeenth and eighteenth centuries in local flint and stone rubble, rendered against the weather. The white weather-boarding on the lane frontage is characteristic of cottages and small houses in Kent and Sussex, many of which were embellished in this way after imported softwoods became widely available in Georgian times. Later additions include a brick extension containing Virginia's bedroom, which the Woolfs built onto the north end of the house, and the large conservatory which they added on the garden side. Still filled with plants, this jungly hothouse casts a watery green light over the ground floor.

ða

Clouds Hill

Dorset

———

O N A sandy Dorset heath, hemmed in by broom and rhododendrons, stands the tiniest of cottages. Built of whitewashed brick, with a hipped slate roof, it is neither pretty nor old, and the front door is curiously set in a windowless wall. Only a smattering of Greek on the shallow pediment above the door suggests it may be more interesting than it looks. Loosely translated as 'why worry', this quote from Herodotus was added by T. E. Lawrence, Lawrence of Arabia, who bought Clouds Hill in 1925, planning to retire here after he left the Royal Air Force. Essentially a one-up, one-down, with a cabin-like bedroom over a spartan bathroom adding another half room on each floor, the inside is still largely as he had it. Apart from the stark bathroom, there are no conveniences. An extendable arm fixed to a fender for making toast is the only concession to cooking; his bed is a built-in bunk below a porthole window; rooms are lit by candles. In Lawrence's day, too, the rhododendron bushes stood in for a privy at the end of the garden.

Clouds Hill is the bolthole of a solitary ascetic. While stationed at nearby Bovington camp, Lawrence would come out here in the evenings to write, read or just sit by the fire, or to host one of his all-male gatherings. It was while on his way back from the camp on his motorcycle, in February 1935, just a few weeks after he retired, that he was killed in an accident.

Flint Cottage · Box Hill

Surrey

———

THIS ENCHANTING Georgian box, with a steep garden running up behind, sits on the slopes of Box Hill, where the chalk downs rise dramatically above Dorking and the River Mole. More villa than cottage, with a classical frontage faced in local flint and brick, it is a charming blend of vernacular materials and architect-inspired design. This is where the novelist George Meredith lived for the last half of his life, from 1867 until his death in 1909. Meredith referred to the little house as a 'hatbox', but he loved its setting and the scenery of the downs: 'I am every morning at the top of Box Hill … I breathe fine air. I shout ha ha to the gates of the world. Then I descend and know myself a donkey for doing it.' He had married for the second time (in Mickleham church down the hill) a few years before he took the cottage, and it was his long-suffering wife who paid for the little chalet high up in the garden, where he retreated to write, and increasingly stayed to sleep.

When Meredith became the grand old man of the English literary scene, Flint Cottage became something of a place of pilgrimage, the promising young men who flocked here including Robert Louis Stevenson and James Barrie. Another frequent visitor was Leslie Stephen, father of Virginia Woolf, who organized Sunday tramps on the downs and brought his tired and hungry companions here for supper before catching a train back to town.

HARDY'S COTTAGE · HIGHER BOCKHAMPTON

Dorset

DOWN A quiet sandy lane off the busy A35 to Dorchester is the secluded cottage where Thomas Hardy was born in 1840. A long low building of cob and thatch, the cottage is typical of many found throughout Dorset, Somerset and Devon. Deep thatch eaves arch over the upper casements, the front door, with its rose-smothered porch, is pleasingly off-centre, and the whole thing is set off by a cheerful burgeoning garden, with narrow paths between overflowing beds. The oldest part, to the left, was built in 1800 by Hardy's great-grandfather as a tiny one-down, two-up, with traditional cob walls two feet thick, made of a pudding of local chalk and clay mixed with straw, and a wheat-straw thatch. The lower, southern half, originally a separate dwelling, is a later extension, while the brick frontage is just a facing to keep the cob in place. Old-fashioned for its date, this is a place of tiny low-ceilinged rooms with deep window seats. Limestone flags from the nearby Isle of Portland floor the main room, and there is a primitive ladder staircase at one end of the house. Woodland presses close, and it is easy to imagine the ponies and deer that looked in at the family through the windows, and the snakes and lizards that found their way over the threshold. Here Hardy gained his empathy with the natural world, and here he returned throughout his life.

ᕦᕤ

OAKHURST COTTAGE · HAMBLEDON
Surrey

———

IN THE nineteenth century, a group of artists began to turn out landscapes that reflected a nostalgic rose-tinted vision of the countryside. Among them was Helen Allingham, whose move to Surrey in 1881 was followed by a stream of delicate and seductive watercolours of attractively decaying buildings and colourful gardens. Oakhurst Cottage, just a mile or so from her home at Witley, was one of the places that caught her eye. With its crooked timber frame, climbers round the door and undulating tiled roof, it is typical of many cottages in this once timber-rich part of the world, and, although altered, probably dates back to the late sixteenth or early seventeenth century. So small that it seems almost like a plaything for children, the cottage is thought to have started life as a barn and was originally just one room open to the rafters. The upper floor with its dormer windows was a later addition, and was probably originally reached by ladder. Now there are stairs, but these lead directly into one of the tiny bedrooms, as was common in such a humble cottage. More unusually, Oakhurst has survived unmodernized. The hearth in the living room is the only source of heat, and out of sight is a traditional earth privy. Today, all is more spruce than it appears in Allingham's painting, which shows flapping washing, pecking chickens, and a woman, babe in arms, at the garden gate.

CHERRYBURN
Northumberland

———

ANOTHER SEDUCTIVE recorder of the countryside was Thomas Bewick (1753–1828), whose finely detailed wood engravings captured the creatures and rural life of his native Northumberland. This little stone cottage attached to his father's smallholding in the Tyne valley is where he was born and brought up. Built of roughly shaped blocks of local sandstone with a stone-flagged ground floor, it is typical of the simple rugged buildings found all over the north of England. In Bewick's day it was rather larger than it appears now. In the 1830s, the family built themselves a substantial farmhouse across the yard, and the old cottage, with one bedroom above three lower rooms, was converted into stables and partly demolished. Originally, it would have been thatched, but with heather from the hills rather than straw. Cut in autumn when it was flowering, the heather could be sheared to a smooth finish and, in the persistent damp of moorland regions, was less likely to rot than straw.

Bewick's talent, fuelled by what he observed on his daily walk to school across the Tyne valley, emerged early, with the flagstones of the cottage floor standing in for a sketching pad. 'Misspending his time in idle pursuits', his father called it, but at fourteen the boy was apprenticed to a Newcastle engraver.

WILLY LOTT'S COTTAGE · FLATFORD
Suffolk

———

THIS MUST be one of the most familiar cottages in England. Part of the scatter of buildings around Flatford Mill, in the peaceful understated valley of the Stour, its tall chimneys, whitewashed gable ends and red-tiled roof have been immortalized by John Constable (1776–1837) in *The Hay-wain* and other paintings. Known as Willy Lott's cottage, after the farmer who once lived here, it is in fact a substantial timber-framed farmhouse, dating from the early seventeenth century and of a kind found throughout the formerly well-wooded countryside of southern and central Suffolk. Unlike the tradition in the Welsh borders, where the framing is often left exposed, houses in this part of the world, from the sixteenth century onwards, were usually given a coating of colour-washed plaster or weather-boarding, with some of them subsequently dignified with an eighteenth-century brick frontage. Across the mill pool in front of the cottage is a substantial brick corn mill, built in 1733 and once owned by Constable's father.

The family lived about a mile away, in an impressive Georgian house in East Bergholt. All the subjects of Constable's Stour paintings lie within a radius of seven miles or so from the village, well within comfortable walking distance.

❧

LAWES COTTAGE · DINTON
Wiltshire

————

THIS HANDSOME stone cottage in the Wiltshire village of Dinton, its limestone walls spotted with lichen, is associated with the Jacobean composer Henry Lawes (1595–1662). Now little known, in his day Lawes entranced the Stuart Court with settings of verses by Jonson, Herrick, Sidney and other poets of the period. And Dinton, only eight miles from Salisbury with its formidable musical reputation, and only five from Wilton House, where the Earls of Pembroke were generous patrons of the arts, seems the perfect place for an aspiring seventeenth-century musician. However, although Henry's father married a Dinton lass and Henry himself was born and christened in the village, his connection with this cottage is shadowy. In 1602 the family moved to Salisbury, where his father was appointed to the cathedral choir, and Henry's own career took him to Court and to a house in Westminster Abbey Close, where he died, as Pepys' diary records.

Henry remembered the poor of Dinton in his will, and perhaps this cottage, which dates from no earlier than the mid seventeenth century, was built for his retirement; it is certainly the kind of substantial building that would have belonged to a man of means. The mullioned windows and carved drip-moulds show the long persistence of medieval practices, and the steeply pitched roof suggests that the cottage was originally thatched, with deep eaves overhanging the upper windows.

Tŷ Mawr · Penmachno
Gwynedd

———

Iɴ 1588, the year Drake scattered the Spanish Armada, the first Welsh Bible was published. This revolutionary translation, which set a new standard for the written language and is still, with minor changes, the version of the Bible in use in Wales today, was the work of Bishop William Morgan (*c.* 1541–1604), who was born in this isolated spot on the eastern side of the Snowdon massif.

Known as Tŷ Mawr, this simple rough-walled dwelling with its deep-set windows, massive chimneys, slate roof and stone-flagged ground floor is typical of Wales's scattered upland farms and cottages: unsophisticated, often crudely built, and constructed of dark-toned, ancient rocks. And this is slate country par excellence, with the great quarries at Dinorwic and Penrhyn just a few miles north-west across the mountains. Even in the late twentieth century, the cottage is still remote, set in wooded farmland at the head of the secluded Wybrnant valley. The hills rise above, with a great stretch of open moorland around Llyn Conwy just a couple of miles to the south. Alas, this little house, typical of those built in this part of Wales after *c.*1560, and now restored to its probable sixteenth-century appearance, almost certainly postdates the bishop's childhood. Although this is the valley where the cleric was born and grew up, he knew an earlier building, which is long gone.

❧

STEPHENSON'S BIRTHPLACE • WYLAM
Northumberland

———

GEORGE STEPHENSON, whose *Rocket* paved the way for steam-driven railways, was born in 1781 in this stone cottage on the banks of the Tyne. Now green and rural, in the eighteenth century this stretch of the valley was an industrial slum of coal pits, ironworks and slag heaps. Coal was king, with a steady stream of boats carrying it south to London. George's father, a colliery worker, was too poor to send any of his children to school, and George started work at about the age of ten, driving one of the horses that pulled the coal-wagons along wooden tramways to the river. The cottage looks substantial enough, but the Stephensons had to share it with three other families, and the two rooms they were given had bare clay floors and unplastered walls. In these early industrial communities, colliery owners took on the feudal power of the lord of the manor, cramming their workers into tied accommodation and often providing shop, pub and chapel as well. Some, such as the Gregs of Styal (see p.84), practised a kind of hard-nosed paternalism that was relatively enlightened; others divided and subdivided their cottages and were indifferent to their workers' welfare. This early industry was rural rather than urban, with villages turned into slums almost overnight by the advent of the mine and the mill. At Wylam, all has been cleaned up, and a riverside walk now follows the route of the former tramway.

INDEX